FLORENCE

Restaurants

The Food Enthusiast's Long Weekend Guide

Andrew Delaplaine

Andrew Delaplaine is the Food Enthusiast.
When he's not playing tennis,
he dines anonymously
at the Publisher's (sometimes considerable) expense.

Copyright © by Gramercy Park Press - All rights reserved.

Please submit corrections, additions or comments to
gppress@gmail.com

The Food Enthusiast's Long Weekend Guide

Table of Contents

Introduction – 5

Getting Around – 15

The A to Z Listings – 17
Ridiculously Extravagant
Sensible Alternatives
Quality Bargain Spots

MARKETS – 69

COOKING SCHOOLS – 73

Index – 77

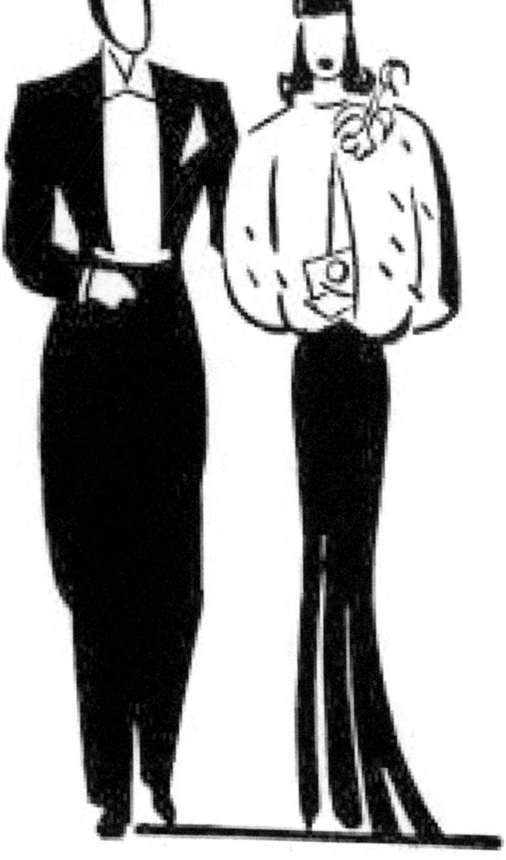

INTRODUCTION

Florence (Firenze), a must-visit destination, is one of the most important historical cities in the world, certainly in the Western world. It is indisputably the cradle of the Renaissance. This is the city where Michelangelo, da Vinci, Botticelli, Galileo and Giotti walked. Besides being the city that was founded by Julius Caesar, Florence is a beautiful city of churches, museums, palaces, and some of the greatest artistic treasures in the world. Travelers from around the globe visit Florence for the beauty of the city and the surrounding hills and towns. One cannot walk the streets of Florence without visiting the **Cathedral, the Baptistery, the Uffizi, the Bargello,** and **the Accademia**. The majesty of the churches of **Santa Maria Novella** and **Santa Croce** must be seen and the **Library of San Lorenzo** is an incredible display of Michelangelo's architectural genius. Florence boasts incredible art collections and monuments for those into history and art, but it's also a city for shoppers and foodies, which is my focus in this book.

I will not soon forget when as a teenager I first visited this town. It was winter and the streets were relatively empty. I knew just enough about art history to know where to go and what to see. I was so captivated by that original visit that I have returned countless times, discovering something each and every time.

So will you.

CUISINE

Italians are passionate about many things especially food. Fiorentini or Tuscan food is simple comfort food and they have adapted a "waste not, want not" philosophy. Basic cuisine consists of bread, olive oil, beef or game, fresh vegetables and wine. Tuscans are also known for their love of beans – a staple of the Tuscan table. Italians love to eat and there are many great places to enjoy the many varieties of Italian cuisine from pizza to fine dining. When searching for

David by Donatello in the Bargello

restaurants, do your research. Many places are closed on Mondays. Remember, traditional Tuscan cuisine incorporates fresh, local ingredients that are simply cooked. Pastas, steaks, seafood, all topped with velvety Tuscan wines. From holes in the walls and cafes to fine dining in posh hotels, Florence is a buffet of dining opportunities. Because of Florence's popularity with tourists, there's a larger group of mediocre restaurants than you find in most Italian towns. Lunch begins around 1 p.m. and dinner begins around 8 p.m. Since most of Florence's restaurants are small, reservations are recommended. The streets are filled with stands serving a variety of culinary adventures like the tripe sandwich. Wine bars flourish in Florence and offer excellent opportunities to take a break from wandering the streets. Enjoy some excellent Chiantis and Tucans from local labels. There's also a sampling of ethnic eateries – usually hit-or-miss. Pizza in Florence is not as good as in Rome or Naples. Small cafes are abundant offering simple menus of coffee drinks, pastries, and panini.

While you're wandering the streets, sample the sandwiches at **NERBONE**, at **FLORENCE'S CENTRAL MARKET**, where the locals line up daily. And the locals do line up for good meals, so if you see a line – it's probably a gem. **TRATTORIA SOSTANZA**, a favorite eatery open since 1869, offers a great selection of Italian treats from bistecca alla fiorentina to the artichoke tart. If you're on the go, stop by '**INO** for a grab-and-go panini. **TRATTORIA MARIO**, another local's favorite that's always packed, is known for serving the best

Central Market / Mercado Centrale

bistecca alla fiorentina's in town. Italians love gelato and it's a perfect snack after any meal or in-between museum visits. Visit **GELATERIA GARABE** for their creamy gelato concoctions and Neopolitan ricotta cake. If you're craving a burger, stop by **POLPA BURGER TRATTORI** where they serve American-style gourmet burgers and pizza. Florence is a giant-mashup of old and new like **LA BOTTEGA DEL BUON CAFÉ**, a modern restaurant housed in a 16th-century medieval building.

CULTURE & ART

Florence is a city of old world charm, seemingly unchanged and filled with artistic masterpieces, colored marbles, and architectural works that reflect the glory of the art and culture of the Renaissance. Called the capital of arts, approximately 60% of the world's most important works of art are located in Italy and about half of these are in Florence. The Italian Renaissance began in Florence when the artist Brunelleschi completed the **Duomo**, with the huge dome. Today Florence is a living museum with its many Renaissance palaces and squares like the **Piazza della Signoria** exhibiting many famous statues and fountains. The chapels, galleries and museums are overflowing with treasures like Florence's most famous museum, the **Uffizi** which houses works by Botticelli, Leonardo da Vinci, Michelangelo, Titan and Rubens. Other museums not to miss include: The **Pitti Palace, Galleria dell'Accademia** and **Palazzo Vecchio.** Some of the grandest churches in Italy are found in Florence including the famous **Duomo of Florence**.

Florence is also a city of incomparable indoor pleasures, capturing the complex, often elusive spirit of the Renaissance more fully than any other place in the country. The most famous museum in Florence is the **Uffizi** which houses works by Botticelli, Leonardo da Vinci, Michelangelo, Titian and Rubens. Other great art museums include **the Pitti Palace, Galleria dell'Accademia** (where you'll find Michelangelo's David) and Palazzo Vecchio. Florence is also home to some of the biggest churches in Italy, including the famous Duomo of Florence.

Florence, an active center of art and culture, presents a series of annual exhibitions, art festivals, and street

Pitti Palace

fairs that fill the city streets with activity. Florence's theaters attract crowds with performances of opera, ballet, and music. During the summer months, Florence is known for outdoor cinemas that project the films on a screen on the façade of a villa. Summers in Florence are festive and the squares and plazas are all brimming with entertainment and local refreshments.

ATTRACTIONS & LANDMARKS

Florence is a great city for walking with the squares and plazas filled with statues and fountains, elegant buildings and shops. Florence can be a bit overwhelming because there's so much to see. Here are some of the attractions that should not be missed.

Medici Chapel

The **Medici Chapel** (Piazza di Madonna degli Aldobrandini, designed by Michelangelo and holds two of his most revered sculptures, "Night and Day" and "Dawn and Dusk." The **Piazzale Michelangelo**, a large square located across the Arno River, offers visitors a magnificent view over the city. The **Boboli Gardens**, located behind the **Palazzo Pitti**, is home to a large number of statues and fountains. Set in the center of the city's main market district, the **Basilica di San Lorenzo** is one of the oldest churches of Florence. The **Baptistery of John the Baptist**, one of Florence's oldest buildings, features an exterior made of green and white marble with three sets of bronze doors. The **Campanile** Bell Tower, in **Piazza del Duomo**, is a popular stop for visitors who enjoy climbing the 414 stairs (no elevator) for great views

Ponte Vecchio

of Florence. Built in 1345, the **Ponte Vecchio** was Florence's first bridge across the Arno River and is lined with shops selling gold and silver jewelry. Located in Piazza Santa Croce, **Santa Croce** is the largest Franciscan church is Italy with tombs that hold famous Florentines like Michelangelo and Dante. This church is known for its beautiful stained glass windows and frescoes.

SHOPPING

Florence offers some of the best shopping opportunities in all of Europe with its thriving open air markets selling everything from food and jewelry to antiques. The most famous market is around **Piazza San Lorenzo** where you'll find an assortment of items including beautiful leather goods. Italy is known for its leathers and Florence offers a variety of leather goods shops. Another popular place is

Mercato Nuovo on Via Porta Rossa, a great place for food shopping and browsing. Name designers like **Gucci** and **Prada**, have outlet shops in Florence offering high end products at more affordable prices. The streets are filled with family-owned boutiques and shops, many offering unique one-of-a-kind gifts and wares. One such shop is **Bartolucci**, in Via Condotta, selling beautiful hand-made wooden toys.

GETTING AROUND

Florence is indeed a walking city, filled with many squares, plazas, fountains, alleyways, and courtyards. There's so much to see walking the streets of Florence but because of the uneven flagstone, sensible shoes should be worn. Many choose to travel by bicycle or scooter and taxis are readily available. Trying to drive in Florence can be taxing because of the city is a maze of one-way streets and pedestrian zones.

Orson Welles once said, "In Italy, for 30 years under the Borgias, they had warfare, terror, murder and bloodshed, but they produced Michelangelo, Leonardo da Vinci and the Renaissance. In Switzerland they had brotherly love, they had 500 years of democracy and peace – and what did it produce? The cuckoo clock."

Here you'll see why Welles was right on the money.

The A to Z Listings
Ridiculously Extravagant
Sensible Alternatives
Quality Bargain Spots

TASTE FLORENCE
http://tasteflorence.com/
I heartily recommend this walking tour of Florence if it's your first time here and you have the time to spare. (Tours run 3 to 5 hours, depending, and the groups are small, between 5 and 15 people.) A guide will take you around the heart of Florence, stopping every 10 or 15 minutes so you can taste the products of local bakeries, chocolate shops, gelaterias, market stalls, street vendors, wine bars. You'll start (probably) at the San Lorenzo Market and head out from that point. The stops at the market stalls are particularly good, mainly because they know which ones to go to and which ones to avoid. So you'll get the best of everything. Another good thing is they don't drag you to a restaurant where you sit down and eat. You walk all over getting little bites here, a glass

of wine there, a cup of coffee here, and so forth. Well worth your time. Fees are very reasonable.

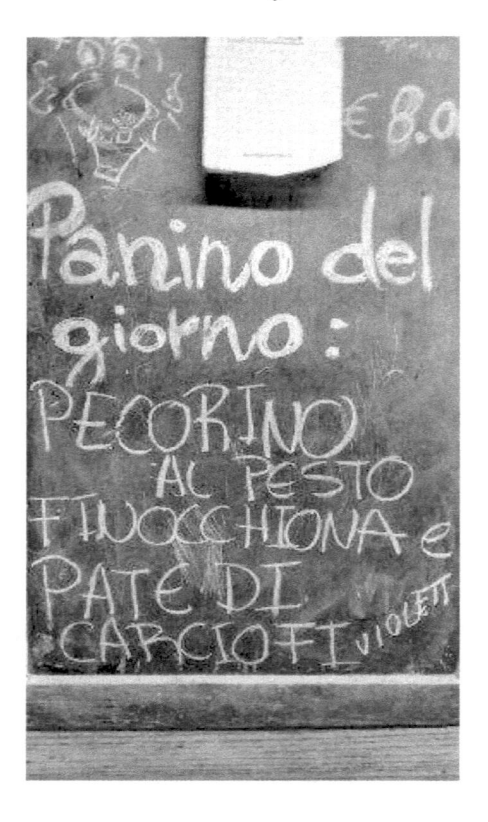

'INO
Via Georgofili 3, Florence, +39 055 214154
www.inofirenze.com/
CUISINE: Sandwiches
DRINKS: Beer & Wine Only
SERVING: 11 a.m. – 5 p.m.
PRICE RANGE: $$
NEIGHBORHOOD: Duomo

Tucked away in a side alley, this place has great panini ('ino is a nickname for panino) made with the freshest focaccia and the finest complementary ingredients, like cured meats, cheeses, grilled veggies, salty marinated fish. The dressings are spectacularly flavorful—truffles, saffron, tart vinegar-based, or a sweeter version, etc. Unless you have something particular in mind, get the daily special. It is probably something you'd never have tried otherwise. Nice house wine.

5 E CINQUE
Piazza della Passera 1, Florence, +39 055 2741583
www.5ecinque.it
CUISINE: Ligurian / Vegetarian
DRINKS: Beer & Wine Only
SERVING: Lunch/Dinner/Closed Monday
PRICE RANGE: $$
NEIGHBORHOOD: Palazzo Pitti

Healthy dining at its best with a menu of salads, pastas, risottos and delicious vegetarian dishes like the Eggplant parmigiana or the chickpea pancakes. They even sell organic wines by the glass. Reservations recommended.

ALL' ANTICO RISTORI DI CAMBI
Via S. Onofrio, 1R, Florence, +39 055 217134
www.anticoristorodicambi.it/
CUISINE: Tuscan
DRINKS: Beer & Wine
SERVING: Lunch/Dinner; closed Sunday
PRICE RANGE: $$$
NEIGHBORHOOD: Palazzo Pitti
Popular restaurant run by the Cambi family since the 1950s dishing up authentic Tuscan fare. They're particularly known for their steaks. Nice selection of pastas, of course, such as the delectable ribollita. Large selection of wines. Menu is all in Italian but the waiter can help you through it.

ANTICA PASTICCERIA SIENI
Via Via Sant'Antonino, 29/R, Florence, +39 055 213830
San Lorenzo Market
www.pasticceriasieni.it
CUISINE: Chocolatier
DRINKS: Full Bar
SERVING: Daytime hours
PRICE RANGE: $$
NEIGHBORHOOD: Santa Maria Novella
Small bar that offers great Italian pastries and coffees. The specialty is traditional Florentine pastries that all

the worker bees in the San Lorenzo Market drink every day. Since 1909, this place has been dishing out the kind of basic food that keep Florence running day in and day out. You'll love it.

ARÀ
Via degli Alfani 127, Florence, +39 055 292548
www.araesicilia.it/
CUISINE: Sicilian
DRINKS: Beer & Wine Only
SERVING: Lunch & Dinner; closed Tuesday
PRICE RANGE: $$$

NEIGHBORHOOD: Duomo
Nice café with a menu of vegetarian and fish options and of course great Sicilian favorites, like the rice balls with different fillings, or the small pizzas cut in half and filled with various stuffings. Don't leave without trying the house made gelato or the cassata.

BORGO ANTICO
Piazza Santo Spirito 6R, Florence, +39 055 210437
www.borgoanticofirenze.com
CUISINE: Italian/Pizza
DRINKS: Full bar
SERVING: Lunch & Dinner
PRICE RANGE: $$

NEIGHBORHOOD: Palazzo Pitti
Perfect place for a quick alfresco lunch. Menu is basically salads, pizza, pastas and risottos. Their Pesto Penne Pasta is the best. Great place for dining away from the touristy sections of town.

BRAC
Via dei Vagellai 18R, Florence, +39 055 0944877
www.libreriabrac.net
CUISINE: Café/Vegetarian
DRINKS: Full Bar
SERVING: Breakfast, Lunch & Dinner
PRICE RANGE: $$
NEIGHBORHOOD: Duomo
Unique library bar (or you could say literary caffè) with a nice menu. Look twice as you pass the address because it's easy to miss this place. In good weather, you can enjoy the lovely courtyard. Inside, the dining

room has lots of bookshelves stuffed to overflowing with art books, and more. Great Sunday brunch. Regular menu offers a la carte or a prix fixe with three tastings. Menu picks: Spinach lasagna and Cabbage salad. Healthy desserts. Reservations recommended. Remember, there's no sign outside.

CAFFÈ AMERINI
Via della Vigna Nuova 61R, Florence, +39 055 284941
CUISINE: Caffè
DRINKS: Full bar
SERVING: Breakfast, Lunch & Dinner
PRICE RANGE: $
NEIGHBORHOOD: Santa Maria Novella
Cute little caffè with a simple menu of salads, pastas, and desserts. You don't actually order from the menu. You choose from what's displayed in the glass display cases and take your seat. Since this very reasonably priced caffè is so close to the fancy shops in the Via de'Tornabuoni, you'll find a lot of shop clerks eat here. They're all dressed to the max. I see the same sort of thing in Bal Harbour in Miami when I'm at Carpaccio. All the nicely dressed clerks sit at the bar (where I do), order soup, and have a cheap lunch. Nice variety of sandwiches and pastries. Staff speaks English.

CAFFÈ CIBREO
Via del Verrocchio 5R, Florence, +39 055 2345853
www.cibreo.com
CUISINE: Italian
DRINKS: Beer & Wine Only

SERVING: Breakfast, Lunch & Dinner; closed Sun & Mon
PRICE RANGE: $$$
NEIGHBORHOOD: Santa Croce
Popular eatery serving up Italian favorites: Menu picks: Liver pate and ricotta and Stuffed Rabbit. Delicious assortment of desserts like the Bavarian fruit tart. Extensive tea selection

CAFFE DELL'ORO
Lungarno degli Acciaiuoli, 4, +39 055 2726 8912
https://www.lungarnocollection.com/caffe-dell-oro/
CUISINE: Mediterranean/Italian
DRINKS: No Booze
SERVING: Breakfast, Lunch & Dinner
PRICE RANGE: $$$$
NEIGHBORHOOD: Duomo
Offering all-day service is this Michelin Italian upscale bistro serving classic Florentine cuisine. The outdoor seating makes it perfect for a splashy lunch.

My Favorites: Salmon Tartare and Filet Mignon. **Incredible views of the Ponte Vecchio,** which makes it an excellent choice for a romantic date night. This is one of those places that has the look and almost tactile "feel" that seems to embody the entire town. It's not a place you will soon forget after you visit. Impressive wine list. Reservations recommended.

CAFFÈ RICCHI
Piazza Santo Spirito 9R, Florence, +39 055 280830
www.ristorantericchi.com/caffericchi/
CUISINE: Italian
DRINKS: Full bar
SERVING: Breakfast, Lunch & Dinner; closed Sunday
PRICE RANGE: $$
NEIGHBORHOOD: Palazzo Pitti
Welcoming caffè away from the tourist scene. Here you'll find nice homecooked Italian fare – menu changes daily. Waiters speak minimal English. Great place for people watching on the charming piazza. They have a restaurant next door at #8R that only serves dinner.

CANTINETTA DEI VERRAZZANO
Via dei Tavolini 18R, Florence, +39 055 268590
www.verrazzano.com
CUISINE: Bakery
DRINKS: Beer & Wine Only
SERVING: 8 a.m. – 9 p.m.
PRICE RANGE: $$
NEIGHBORHOOD: Duomo

More than just a bakery, this place serves a variety of coffees – perfect espressos, macchiatos, and lattes, but also great selection of focaccia breads, hams, cheeses, and pastries. They also offer gluten-free items. Great wine selection. Only a few tables so you may have a little wait.

CARABÈ
Via Ricasoli 60R, Florence, +39 055 289476
www.parcocarabe.it
WEBSITE DOWN AT PRESSTIME
CUISINE: Ice Cream/Frozen Yogurt
DRINKS: No Booze
SERVING: 9 a.m. - Midnight
PRICE RANGE: $

NEIGHBORHOOD: Duomo
This place specializes in Sicilian gelato – no eggs or cream. They only use seasonal ingredients, too, which makes everything much fresher. Great cannoli – made to order, but only if you ask because they're not in the glass cases.

CASA DEL VINO
Via dell'Ariento 16R, Florence, +39 055 215609
www.casadelvino.it
CUISINE: Bar / Wine Bar
DRINKS: Full bar
SERVING: Breakfast & Lunch; closed Sunday
PRICE RANGE: $

NEIGHBORHOOD: Santa Maria Novella
This dark-wooded and welcoming wine bar is a great place to duck into to escape the pulsing crowds of the San Lorenzo Market. Stand at the bar to order a quick lunch and choose from lots of bottles served by the glass. (They even have their own Prosecco, which is very good, by the way.) They serve up delicious panini (you can choose which kind of bread they use) and the crostini are excellent as well.

CIBREO TEATRO DEL SALE
Via del Verrocchio, 2r, Florence, +39 055 2477881
www.cibreo.com
CUISINE: Italian
DRINKS: Full bar
SERVING: Lunch/Dinner/Late Night
PRICE RANGE: $
NEIGHBORHOOD: Santa Croce
This is a treat for the taste buds. Creative tasting menu offering 16 courses. Food is cooked in front of you, plated and served. It's all a heady mix of cuisines, from Korean to Italian, to Chinese and Japanese. Favorites: Baozi and Tortellini. Nice selection of wines and desserts. Delicious Italian fare in a charming eatery featuring high ceilings and dramatic food. Everything from the little anchovy sandwiches to the delectable pastries is excellent. Sit outside in good weather.

COQUINARIUS
Via dell'Oche 11R, Florence, +39 055 2302153
www.coquinarius.it
CUISINE: Italian

DRINKS: Beer & Wine Only
SERVING: Lunch & Dinner
PRICE RANGE: $$$$
NEIGHBORHOOD: Duomo
Charming eatery offering creative Italian fare, over a dozen robust salads and great crostini. Seasonal kitchen and sophisticated though casual wine bar with lower than average prices. Menu favorites: Tagliatelle with rabbit and Smoked Salmon. Incredible wine list.

DA NERBONE
MERCATO CENTRALE
Piazza del Mercato Centrale, +39 339 648 0251
No website
East Corner of the Market.
CUISINE: Tuscan/Sandwiches
DRINKS: No Booze

SERVING: Breakfast & Lunch; Closed Sun
PRICE RANGE: $
NEIGHBORHOOD: Santa Maria Novella
Classic institution serving traditional Tuscan cuisine for nearly a century-and-a-half. This part of the Mercato centrale is closed for dinner, so breakfast or lunch are your only options, and either one you choose will be good. The place is ultra-casual. I find the place a little rough-and-tumble, but the food is spectacular. My Favorites: Tuscan Stew and Lampredotto with hot chili sauce.

DOLCI & DOLCEZZE
Piazza Beccaria Cesare 8R, Florence, +39 055 2345458
No Website
CUISINE: Chocolatier/Pastries
SERVING: 9 – 7:30; closed Sunday

PRICE RANGE: $$$
NEIGHBORHOOD: Santa Croce
Little pastry shop selling delicious Italian sweets, tartes, chocolate and fruit tortes, and great coffees. Definitely get something made with chocolate at this place.

ENOTECA PINCHIORRI
Via Ghibellina, 87, +39 055 242777
https://www.enotecapinchiorri.it/
CUISINE: Italian
DRINKS: Full Bar
SERVING: Dinner, Late Night, Closed Sun & Mon
PRICE RANGE: $$$$
NEIGHBORHOOD: Florence Historic Center
Luxury Michelin-starred eatery serving traditional Tuscan fare prepared and served with the most exacting care. Most people who know what they're

talking about (and I'm one of them), consider this not only the best restaurant in Florence, but at the same time the most expensive. But I stand by my general feeling that most 3-star spots like this are precious to the point of boredom. While I *do* look forward to the food here and the exquisite service, I'm always a little disappointed by the *experience*—I don't like the idea of going to church to eat, maybe that's it. My Favorites: Ravioli with swiss chard and Spaghetti alla chitarra with seafood. Extensive wine list. Reservations recommended.

GELATERIA DEI NERI
Via dei Neri 9, Florence, +39 055 210034
https://gelateriadeineri.it/

CUISINE: Ice Cream/Frozen Yogurt/Gelato
DRINKS: No Booze
SERVING: 9 a.m. - Midnight
PRICE RANGE: $
NEIGHBORHOOD: Duomo
Authentic Italian gelato and sorbetto with a wide range of flavors. (Try the fig with ricotta.)

GHIBELLINA FORNO
Via Ghibellina 41R, Florence, +39 055 241544
No Website
CUISINE: Bakery
DRINKS: No Booze
SERVING: 7 a.m. – 8 p.m.
PRICE RANGE: $$
NEIGHBORHOOD: Santa Croce
Since 1890, this bakery has been serving freshly baked pastries and savory treats. Try the Nutella-filled croissants. They offer a nice selection of breads, pizzas, and sandwiches.

GILDA
Piazza Ghiberti 41R, Florence, +39 055 2343885
www.gildabistrot.it
CUISINE: Italian
DRINKS: Beer & Wine Only
SERVING: Breakfast, Lunch & Dinner
PRICE RANGE: $$$
NEIGHBORHOOD: Santa Croce
Small but comfortable eatery offering a great selection of authentic Italian fare, much of it bought at the nearby market of Sant'Ambrogio. Reservations recommended. A thoroughly charming place you'll

fall in love with. (There really is a Gilda, and you'll probably meet her when you visit.)

GOLDEN VIEW OPEN BAR
Via de Bardi 58R, Florence, +39 055 214502
www.goldenviewopenbar.com
CUISINE: Italian
DRINKS: Full bar
SERVING: Breakfast, Lunch & Dinner
PRICE RANGE: $$$
NEIGHBORHOOD: Palazzo Pitti
Popular upscale eatery serving delicious Italian fare. (I like the mussels and prawns served with spaghetti.) The name is awkwardly direct, as if the owner said to himself: "How can I get across the point that my terrace has a golden view of the river and the bridge?" and then he came up with this name because it does indeed have splendid views of the Arno and the Ponte Vecchio. Live jazz music. Amazing specialty

cocktails. Make reservations for lunch or dinner. You can have breakfast from 7 at the little café. Lunch from noon.

GUCCI OSTERIA BY MASSIMO BOTTURA
Piazza della Signoria 10, Florence, +39 055 0621744
www.gucci.com/it/it/store/osteria-bottura
CUISINE: Sicilian
DRINKS: Beer & Wine Only
SERVING: Lunch & Dinner
PRICE RANGE: $$$
NEIGHBORHOOD: Duomo
Small café located inside the Gucci Garden offering a menu of iconic Italian dishes. Favorites: Torellin in Parmesan sauce and Hotdogs made with Tuscan Chianina beef. Nice selection of desserts. Diners get free admission to the Gucci Fashion House museum.

GUCCI OSTERIA DA MASSIMO BOTTURA
Piazza della Signoria, 10, +39 055 062 1744
https://www.gucci.com/it/it/store/osteria-bottura

CUISINE: Italian/Contemporary
DRINKS: Full Bar
SERVING: Lunch & Dinner
PRICE RANGE: $$$
NEIGHBORHOOD: Florence Historic Center
Just a tiny hop from the famous Uffizi Gallery inside the Gucci store is this upscale eatery offering tasting menus and a la carte service. My Favorites: Emilia Burger and the iconic Massimo Bottura dish. Reservations recommended.

GURDULU
Via delle Caldaie, 12R, Florence, +39 055 282223
www.gurdulu.com
CUISINE: Italian/Mediterranean
DRINKS: Full Bar
SERVING: Dinner; Lunch on Sat
PRICE RANGE: $$$$
NEIGHBORHOOD: Santo Spirito / San Frediano
Glamorous eatery with an adventurous a la carte menu as well as tasting menu. Favorites: Gnocchi; Amberjack; Quail. There's also a lovely walled in garden. Tasty cocktails – for some the highlight of this place.

HOSTARIA IL DESCO
Via delle Terme, 23/R, +39 055 294882
https://www.hostariaildesco.com/
CUISINE: Italian/Tuscan
DRINKS: Beer & Wine
SERVING: Lunch & Dinner
PRICE RANGE: $$
NEIGHBORHOOD: Duomo

A very classy, elegant eatery offering authentic Italian fare. It's down one of those narrow alleys that could be called a street 500 years ago but is an alley today. After you leave the hustle and bustle of the surging hoards at the Ponte Vecchio, you'll come to this wonderful spot frequented by locals more than tourists. My Favorites: the lovely Veal Chop; the Gnocchi with Gorgonzola and pear (sheer heaven); the Mozzarella Marinara Gnocchi; the cheesecake for dessert is the best—light & fluffy. You don't feel like you're really eating cheesecake. Impressive wine list. Gluten free selections.

I DUE FRATELLINI
Via dei Cimator 38R, Florence, +39 055 239 6096
www.iduefratellini.it
WEBSITE DOWN AT PRESSTIME
CUISINE: Sandwiches
DRINKS: Beer & Wine Only
SERVING: Breakfast, Lunch & Dinner
PRICE RANGE: $
NEIGHBORHOOD: Duomo
Great sandwich shop where the star is the assortment of delicious breads used for the sandwiches. Not to mention the staggering array of Panini choices. The last time I was here, I stopped counting at 20 different sandwiches. I wanted them all. The crowd surging around me couldn't have agreed more.

IL BORRO
Lungarno Acciaiuoli 80R, Florence, +39 055 290423
www.ilborrotuscanbistro.it
CUISINE: Tuscan
DRINKS: Beer & Wine Only
SERVING: Lunch & Dinner; closed Monday
PRICE RANGE: $$
NEIGHBORHOOD: Duomo
Popular eatery (owned by the Ferragamo estate) with a seasonal menu including organic chicken crostini, fresh fish and pastas, meat and vegetable plates. A lot of the veggies come from their own farm. Save room for dessert. Nice selection of wines.

IL CERNACCHINO
Via della Condotta 38R, Florence, +39 055 294119
www.ilcernacchio.com/
CUISINE: Sandwiches
DRINKS: Beer & Wine Only
SERVING: Breakfast, Lunch & Dinner (but only till around 7:30)
PRICE RANGE: $$
NEIGHBORHOOD: Duomo

Great family-run lunch spot, and, like so many super spots like thisw that cater to locals in a hurry, you're never lingering long in this place, though it's great fun to hang aput and just watch everything bustling around you. Menu offers a selection of fresh panini, Italian snacks, salads, risottos, you name it. They have a dish they made famous, which involves a hollowed out roll stuffed with your choice of meatballs, sausage & greens or tripe. (Don't get the tripe!)

IL MERCATO CENTRALE
Piazza del Mercato Centrale 4, Florence, +39 055 2399798
www.mercatocentrale.it
CUISINE: Italian/Steakhouse
DRINKS: Beer & Wine Only
SERVING: Lunch & Dinner
PRICE RANGE: $$
NEIGHBORHOOD: Santa Maria Novella
Two-level venue: first floor is a market (the old-school San Lorenzo Market) selling meats, cheeses, fish, pastas, fruits and vegetables; and the chic second floor Mercato Centrale, a food hall where you choose from a variety of food stalls manned by professional bakers, butchers, salumi curators and so much more. You'll go nuts here.

Outside at Il Pilagio

IL PILAGIO
FOUR SEASONS HOTEL
Borgo Pinti 99, +39 055 26261
https://www.fourseasons.com/florence/dining/restaurants/il_palagio/
CUISINE: Italian/Mediterranean
DRINKS: Full Bar
SERVING: Lunch & Dinner, Late Night, Brunch
PRICE RANGE: $$$$
NEIGHBORHOOD: Florence Historic Center
Upscale eatery offering regional classics, a tasting menu and wine pairing in one of the most luxurious settings in Florence, and that's saying something. If you can imagine you had the only table in the room, and everybody else disappeared, you will feel like a prince dining in his own villa, so opulent are the furnishings and décor, so attentive and exquisite the service. The Michelin star brings a lot with it, of

course. My Favorites: Seafood Risotto and Marinated Eggplant. Vegetarian friendly. Reservations recommended.

Inside at Il Pilagio

IL SANTO BEVITORE
Via Santo Spirito 64R, Florence, +39 055 211264
www.ilsantobevitore.com
CUISINE: Italian
DRINKS: Beer & Wine
SERVING: Lunch/Dinner
PRICE RANGE: $$$
NEIGHBORHOOD: Palazzo Pitti

Charming restaurant with a beautiful dining room featuring a barrel vaulted ceiling that will make you feel like you're in a small church from 400 years ago. Lunch menu is much less heavy than dinner. And the menus changes every week to reflect what's freshest. Nice selection of Tuscan cheeses and pastas and a wide selection of wines by the glass. (they will do wine tastings for you as well.) Menu favorite: Duck and Wheat spaghetti with squid. Multi-lingual staff. Good choice for lunch or dinner.

KONNUBIO
Via dei Conti, Firenze FI, 39 055 238 1189
www.konnubio.com/it/
CUISINE: Italian
DRINKS: Beer & Wine Only
SERVING: Lunch, Dinner, Brunch
PRICE RANGE: $$$

NEIGHBORHOOD: Duomo
Multi-concept chic eatery offering a variety of cuisines – Tuscan, international, vegan and vegetarian. It's an intimate eatery with a variety of dining options from breakfast at the bar or buffet style, afternoon tea, or an upscale lunch or dinner. Favorites: Braised Veal Cheek and Florentine T-Bone Steak. Extensive wine list.

L'OSTERIA DI GIOVANNI
Via del Moro, 22, +39 055 284897
http://www.osteriadigiovanni.com/
CUISINE: Tuscan
DRINKS: Full Bar
SERVING: Dinner, Lunch & Dinner Sat & Sun

PRICE RANGE: $$$
NEIGHBORHOOD: Santa Maria Novella
Cozy eatery with vintage furniture run by the same family for years—it has an impressive menu of Bruschetta, steaks, and pastas. My Favorites: Pasta with Porcini mushrooms; Braised rabbit with olives; and a delicious Steak Florentine cooked on their charcoal grill, which adds a special taste. Be sure to get the side order of fried Zucchini—it's delicate and sublime. Desserts are tempting but they serve complimentary lemon sorbet and biscotti. Nice wine selection. Reservations required.

LA PICCOLA CORTE
Via Borgognossanti 124R, Florence, +39 055 2691916
No Website
CUISINE: Tuscan
DRINKS: Full Bar
SERVING: Lunch & Dinner
PRICE RANGE: $$
NEIGHBORHOOD: Stazione Ferroviaria/Santa Maria Novella
Creative menu of Italian fare. Favorites: Pica Pasta and Crispy Speck & Nuts. Save room for the delicious tiramisu. Impressive list of Tuscany wines.

LA CARRAIA
Piazza Nazario Sauro, Florence, +39 055 280695
www.lacarraiagroup.eu
CUISINE: Ice cream/Frozen Yogurt
DRINKS: No Booze
SERVING: 10 a.m. - Midnight

PRICE RANGE: $
NEIGHBORHOOD: Palazzo Pitti
Italian gelato is the best and this place serves light and creamy flavors and large portions. Great flavors like: chocolate, cookies, fig ricotta, passionfruit, black cherry, tiramisu, cheesecake, and raspberry.

LA MENAGERE
Via Ginori 8R, Florence, +39 055 0750600
www.lamenagere.it
CUISINE: Italian
DRINKS: Full Bar
SERVING: Dinner
PRICE RANGE: $$$
NEIGHBORHOOD: Santa Maria Novella
Hip eatery featuring trendy décor, live music and delicious cocktails. Up front you'll find casual dining with a bistro atmosphere, while in the rear is the fine dining section. Favorites: Grilled octopus and Yellow

tail tuna with pesto rocket. Great wine. This place is a combination cocktail bar, café, flower shop and store.

LE BOTTEGHE DI LEONARDO
Via de' Ginori 21R, Florence, +39 388 345 0986
www.lebotteghedileonardo.it/
WEBSITE DOWN AT PRESSTIME
CUISINE: Ice Cream/Frozen Yogurt
SERVING: Lunch/Dinner/Late Night
PRICE RANGE: $
NEIGHBORHOOD: Santa Maria Novella
Italians are known for their gelato and this shop offers some of the best. Great selections of flavors like Melon and Pear. Flavors change often, but the thing to remember about this place is that all the ingredients are from the very best suppliers.

LOBS FISH RESTAURANT
Via Faenza 75R, Florence, +39 055 212478
No Website
CUISINE: Italian
DRINKS: Full bar
SERVING: Lunch/Dinner/Late Night
PRICE RANGE: $$$
NEIGHBORHOOD: Santa Maria Novella
Guests are welcomed with a glass of Prosecco upon seating. Menu offers Italian fare with a focus on seafood. The nautical décor makes you feel like you're sitting by the harborside where they might have caught the fish. Favorites: Linguine with seafood and Seafood Risotto.

MANGIAFOCO
Borgo Santi Apostoli 26R, Florence, +39 055 2658170
www.mangiafoco.com/
CUISINE: Tuscan
DRINKS: Beer & Wine Only
SERVING: Lunch & Dinner; closed Sunday
PRICE RANGE: $$
NEIGHBORHOOD: Duomo
Small place (operated by a husband and wife team) has not only great food and wine, but the most charming friendly atmosphere as well. Try the truffle pasta and beef. Basically a wine bar (large wine list) with a nice menu of appetizers, pasta dishes and a few main courses. The perfect place to relax while trying some new wines along with a charcuterie board. The salumi is excellent. You'll want to drink the olive oil it's so good.

OLIO & CONVIVIUM
Via Santo Spirito 4, Florence, +39 055 2658198
http://oliorestaurant.it/
CUISINE: Italian
DRINKS: Full bar

SERVING: Lunch/Dinner; closed Monday
PRICE RANGE: $$$
NEIGHBORHOOD: Palazzo Pitti
Popular local upscale eatery with great authentic Italian fare and wine pairings. You'll love the dining room with the floor-to-ceiling bookshelves, only there aren't any books on the shelves, just bottles of wine. (I was surprised how charming this simple design idea was the minute I walked in, and that I've never seen it done like this before.) It's a great place watch the chef work in the kitchen. Excellent spot for a

charcuterie platter, and they even do olive oil tastings. Menu picks: Tagliata with porcinis and any of the pastas. Huge wine selection.

OSTERIA CAFFÈ ITALIANO
Via Isola delle Stinche 11R, Florence, +39 055 289080
http://www.caffeitaliano.it
CUISINE: Italian/Wine Bar
DRINKS: Beer & Wine Only
SERVING: Lunch & Dinner
PRICE RANGE: $$
NEIGHBORHOOD: Duomo
Lovely restaurant with a dramatic high ceiling and an intricate chandelier has a menu of traditional Italian fare. Favorites: Eggplant Parm and Tuscan style pizza. Little English spoken here, but you can manage.

OSTERIA CINGHIALE BIANCO
Borgo S. Jacopo, 43, +39 055 215706
http://cinghialebianco.com/home/

CUISINE: Tuscan
DRINKS: Full Bar
SERVING: Dinner, Lunch & Dinner Sat & Sun
PRICE RANGE: $$$
NEIGHBORHOOD: Palazzo Pitti
If you're exhausted after tramping through the endless corridors of the Pitti Palace, make a beeline to this wonderful quaint little spot set in a 14th Century tower. This upscale eatery serves some of the most traditional Tuscan fare (by that I mean authentic) to be found in the area. My Favorites: Pappardelle with wild boar and Steak with Arugula and Parmesan. Vegetarian options.

OSTARIA DEI CENTOPOVERI
Via Palazzuolo 31R, Florence, +39 055 218846
www.centopoveri.it
CUISINE: Pizza/Italian
DRINKS: Beer & Wine Only
SERVING: Lunch & Dinner
PRICE RANGE: $$
NEIGHBORHOOD: Santa Maria Novella
Great place for dinner serving traditional Italian fare and pizzas (though the pizzas aren't served on the weekends). At lunch, they have a very cheap menu giving you 2 courses and wine that you'll find hard to beat anywhere in Florence for this level of quality. (The regular menu is quite large, so there's plenty to choose from.) quite a bit more costly at dinner. Amazing desserts. Very busy so get there early. Waiters speak English.

OSTERIA DI PASSIGNANO
Via Passignano, 33, Badia A Passignano, +39 055 807 1278
http://www.osteriadipassignano.com/
CUISINE: Italian
DRINKS: Beer & Wine
SERVING: Lunch & Dinner, Lunch only on Sun; Closed Mon
PRICE RANGE: $$$$
NEIGHBORHOOD: Chianti Classico region,
Upscale dining at its best with a menu of Italian classics. This place isn't in town, but on the road between Florence and sienna, located in the Tuscan hills. I mention this place because it's just so damned wonderful and picturesque. My Favorites: Tomato Ravioli with pesto and Cornish hen with asparagus. Pre fixe menus with wine pairings or a la cart service. Reservations only.

OSTERIA FRANCESCANA
Via Stella 22, Modena, +02 626 020362

https://osteriafrancescana.it
CUISINE: Sicilian
DRINKS: Full Bar
SERVING: Lunch & Dinner, Dinner only on Saturdays; Closed Sundays
PRICE RANGE: $$$$
NEIGHBORHOOD: Modena

Cute little eatery with a small menu named as the "Best Restaurant in the World" in The World's 50 Best Restaurants. Reservations are hard to get as the chef was featured on Chef's Table and Master of None. Order A la Carte or from the 12 course tasting menu. Favorites: Tortellini and Lobster in double sauce. Reservations needed.

OSTERIA PEPÒ
Via Rosina 4/6R, Florence, +39 055 283259
www.pepo.it
CUISINE: Tuscan
DRINKS: Beer & Wine Only
SERVING: Lunch & Dinner

PRICE RANGE: $$
NEIGHBORHOOD: Santa Maria Novella
How many times have you had the "simple" dish of spaghetti with tomato sauce, garlic, basil? A hundred? A thousand? If there is such a thing as the "right" way to prepare such a simple, basic Italian dish, this is the place to compare everything else you've had against. Best spaghetti I've ever had. Another favorite: Spinach ravioli. The menu changes daily, but there's always that remarkable spaghetti. Nice selection of wines. Delicious desserts. The staff are fun and enthusiastic. Crammed with locals.

PERCHÉ NO!
Via dei Tavolini 19R, Florence, +39 055 2398969
www.percheno.firenze.it
CUISINE: Ice cream/Frozen Yogurt
SERVING: 11- 11
PRICE RANGE: $
NEIGHBORHOOD: Duomo
This is a famous gelateria that's been around since just before World War 2. No preservatives, no emulsifiers, nothing fake in their gelatos. Nice selection of traditional gelato flavors, but also some creamy and flavorful choices like chocolate mint. Lactose free choices.

RINUCCIO 1180
Via Cassia Per Siena 133, Bargino, +39 055 235 9720
www.antinori.it
CUISINE: Italian
DRINKS: Beer & Wine Only
SERVING: Lunch

PRICE RANGE: $$$
NEIGHBORHOOD: Bargino
Gorgeous bistro-style eatery ideal for a late lunch and wine tastings. Creative menu of Italian fare. Favorites: Duck ragout pasta and Chicken breast. Impressive wine selection. Reservations please.

RISTORANTE DA MIMMO
Via San Gallo, 57-59 R, Florence, +39 055 481030
www.ristorantedamimmo.it
CUISINE: Pizza/Mediterranean
DRINKS: Beer & Wine Only
SERVING: Dinner; closed Mondays
PRICE RANGE: $$
NEIGHBORHOOD: Indipendenza
You can beat this location in what used to be a grand old theatre. There's a fresco on the ceiling dating to the 17th Century. There's a liveliness about this place that always draws me back. At lunch they offer what they call a "worker's menu," which includes a pasta, a big salad (insalatone) and a main course. And you can't beat the prices, at lunch anyway. The prices jump quite a bit at dinner, but it's just as fun. Great Italian fare like fresh basil pesto pasta and ricotta cheesecake. Menu picks: Beefsteak Florentine, porchetta. Impressive house wines. Reservations recommended.

RIVOIRE
Piazza Signoria, Florence, +39 055 214412
www.rivoire.it
CUISINE: Desserts/Chocolates/Bar
DRINKS: Full bar
SERVING: Breakfast, Lunch & Dinner
PRICE RANGE: $$$
NEIGHBORHOOD: Duomo
More than just desserts, though this place has been famous (for over a century) for its superior tiramisu and hot chocolate that's topped off with a dollop of freshly whipped cream like none you've ever had before. Excellent choice if you're in the neighborhood in the morning to stop in for your cappuccino and a delectable pastry. They've won prizes for their chocolate creations, and they make them all right here on site. There's also a nice menu of pastas, but you can get pasta anywhere in Florence. The pastries and hot drinks you can only find here. It doesn't hurt that this place is situated on the lovely Piazza Signoria. Wait staff speak English.

ROBIGLIO
Via dei Tosinghi 11R, Florence, +39 055 212784
CUISINE: Café/Ice Cream/Frozen Yogurt
DRINKS: No Booze
SERVING: 9 a.m. – 8 p.m.
PRICE RANGE: $$
NEIGHBORHOOD: Duomo
This old-style pasticceria (dating back to 1928) might be another great place for gelato, but it's also a great place for a snack. Menu features biscotti, quiche and pastries. Breakfast and lunch. Great desserts.

SE STO ON ARNO ROOFTOP
THE WESTIN EXCELSIOR
Piazza Ognissanti, 3, +39 055 27151
https://www.sestoonarno.com
CUISINE: Italian / Lounge
DRINKS: Full Bar
SERVING: Lunch & Dinner; Closed Sat & Sun
PRICE RANGE: $$$$
NEIGHBORHOOD: Santa Maria Novella

Upscale eatery located on the 6th floor of the Westin with two terraces offering some of the most impressive views you're going to find of the city. This is a real gourmet menu, not crappy food with jumped up prices because they have this great view. Still, it's OK to come here just for drinks and the view. (I bring first-timers here so they can enjoy that very view I'm raving about.) Has an extensive wine list. Vegetarian options. Late night dining or just cocktails.

SEI DIVINO
Via Borgo Ognissanti 42R, Florence, +39 351 544 7394
www.seidivinofirenze.it
WEBSITE DOWN AT PRESSTIME
CUISINE: Tuscan
DRINKS: Wines
SERVING: Dinner
PRICE RANGE: $$
NEIGHBORHOOD: Santa Maria Novella
Popular eatery/wine bar attracts a savvy young crowd. Impressive collection of more than 400 different wines. Menu changes daily from pasta to fish (different country every day). Delicious desserts.

SEMEL
Piazza Lorenzo Ghiberti 44R, Florence
No phone/No website
CUISINE: Sandwiches/Tuscan
DRINKS: Beer & Wine Only
SERVING: Lunch
PRICE RANGE: $

NEIGHBORHOOD: Santa Croce
Cute little sandwich shop with only a few stools at the counter. Great panini (roasted pork, duck, chicken, salami, and the sardines I love so much) and sandwiches served on freshly baked bread. Small wine selection, several by the glass. Superior artisanal beers. Staff speak English.

SERGIO GOZZI
Piazza di San Lorenzo 8R, Florence, +39 055 281941
No Website
CUISINE: Tuscan
DRINKS: Beer & Wine Only
SERVING: Lunch; closed Sunday
PRICE RANGE: $$
NEIGHBORHOOD: Santa Maria Novella
Authentic little Trattoria located in an unassuming store front that's been home to the Gozzi family since they started this place in 1915. Communal tables.

Simple menu of rich Tuscan fare that changes daily. Filled with locals, who can't get enough of it.

SHAKE CAFFÈ
Via degli Avelli 2R, Florence, +39 055 906 0597
www.shakecafe.bio/
CUISINE: Caffè
DRINKS: Full Bar
SERVING: 7 a.m. – 8 p.m.
PRICE RANGE: $
NEIGHBORHOOD: Santa Maria Novella
Healthy caffè offering fresh pressed juices, smoothies, coffees, breakfast and lunch. Popular drinks: Vitamin C smoothie and Detox juice. Nice selection of sandwiches. Vegetarian and vegan options. It's a little "too" healthy for my taste, but I was drawn here by a vegan friend who swears by the place. They even have things like soy milk, unheard of anywhere else in town.

TRATTORIA 4 LEONI
Via de' Vellutini 1R, Florence, +39 055 218562
www.4leoni.com
CUISINE: Tuscan
DRINKS: Beer & Wine Only
SERVING: Lunch & Dinner
PRICE RANGE: $$$
NEIGHBORHOOD: Palazzo Pitti
Nice upscale eatery on the Piazza della Passera, and if the weather is nice, by all means sit outside. They have a creative menu of Tuscan fare including salads, pastas, and steaks. There are a couple of standout dishes, like the "fried barnyard," which includes zucchini, eggplant, rabbit, chicken, polenta and potatoes; or the Passera salad, with cabbage, zucchini and avocado. Menu is in Italian but the waiters speak English. Try the cheesecake, it's the best.

TRATTORIA DA ROCCO
Piazza Ghiberti, Florence, +39 339 8384555

https://trattoriadarocco.business.site/
CUISINE: Tuscan
DRINKS: Beer & Wine Only
SERVING: Breakfast & Lunch
PRICE RANGE: $
NEIGHBORHOOD: Santa Croce
Great affordable breakfast and lunch spot located inside the always busy market of Sant'Ambrogio. Menu favorites: Bacala salad and Polpete (meatballs in marinara sauce). Heated buffet. Filled with locals who are looking for tasty food served quickly. You won't be disappointed.

TRATTORIA DEL CARMINE
Piazza del Carmine 18R, Florence, +39 055 218601
No Website
CUISINE: Tuscan
DRINKS: Beer & Wine
SERVING: Lunch/Dinner
PRICE RANGE: $$
NEIGHBORHOOD: Palazzo Pitti
Everything here is authentic and always prepared fresh. It's always easy here to go with the daily specials, which focus on the freshest ingredients available. Favorites: Spaghetti alle vongole and Veal and chips, as well as the expertly prepared Florentine beefsteak. Nice selection of fresh seafood. Nice Italian desserts. Dining inside and on the patio. No AC inside.

TRATTORIA LA CASALINGA
Via dei Michelozzi 9R, Florence, +39 055 218624
www.trattorialacasalinga.it
CUISINE: Tuscan
DRINKS: Full bar
SERVING: Lunch & Dinner; closed Sunday
PRICE RANGE: $
NEIGHBORHOOD: Palazzo Pitti
Comfortable eatery offering delicious authentic, homemade Tuscan food. La Casalinga means "the housewife," so you get the idea what this place is like. Just like home. Favorites: Spaghetti carbonara and Steak with arugula. Menu in Italian and waiters barely speak English, but you'll have a blast in this busy, bustling joint.

TRATTORIA L'PARIONE
Via del Parione 74R, Florence, +39 055 214005
www.parione.net
CUISINE: Italian

DRINKS: Beer & Wine Only
SERVING: Lunch/Dinner/Late Night
PRICE RANGE: $$$
NEIGHBORHOOD: Santa Maria Novella
Upscale eatery serving delicious Italian fare and some of the best pasta you'll ever eat. Favorites: Wild boar pasta and Black truffle gnocchi. Great wine selection.

TRATTORIA MARIONE
Via della Spada 27R, Florence, +39 055 214756
www.casatrattoria.com
CUISINE: Tuscan
DRINKS: Beer & Wine Only
SERVING: Lunch & Dinner
PRICE RANGE: $$
NEIGHBORHOOD: Santa Maria Novella
Typical cuisine of Florence. Amazing T-bone steaks and Fried meatballs and zucchini. Menu favorite: Roasted chicken with rosemary potatoes. Ask the server for suggestions - you can't go wrong. The bread is the best. Come early to avoid the lines. Note: this is a casual dining spot and the meal is never rushed.

TRATTORIA SOSTANZA
Via del Porcellana 25R, Florence, +39 055 212691
No Website
CUISINE: Italian
DRINKS: Beer & Wine Only
SERVING: Lunch, Dinner
PRICE RANGE: $$$
NEIGHBORHOOD: Santa Maria Novella

Located a bit off the beaten path but worth the trouble just for their "Butter Chicken" (Pollo al Burro and Bisteak). It's grilled over hot coals and then dredged in flour and egg batter before hitting the saute pan where it gets cooked in more butter. It's then cooked over coals once more until browned and ready. They serve this incredible dish in the pan it was cooked in. Other dishes include Tortellini, Artichoke pie and Florentine steak. Nice selection of desserts. Reservations a must.

VIVOLI
Via Isola delle Stinche 7R, Florence, +39 055 292334
www.vivoli.it
CUISINE: Pastry/Gelato
DRINKS: No Booze
SERVING: 9 a.m. to 9 p.m.; closed Sunday
PRICE RANGE: $$
NEIGHBORHOOD: Duomo
Busy gelato spot that dates back to 1930. Here you pay first and then take your ticket to the counter to

order. Listed as the #1 gelato spot in Florence. They don't even offer cones, just cups. While they have a wide variety of flavors, a lot of other places do, too. Try the affogato, which is a shot of espresso topping an order of vanilla gelato. As close to heave as you're likely to get.

ZEB
Via S. Miniato, 2r, +39 055 234 2864
http://www.zebgastronomia.com/1148-2/
CUISINE: Tuscan / Wine Bar
DRINKS: Beer & Wine
SERVING: Lunch & Dinner, Lunch only Sun – Tues; Closed Wed
PRICE RANGE: $$$
NEIGHBORHOOD: Michelangelo
Elegant eatery run by a mother and son serving authentic Tuscan cuisine. Forget all about the menu. Order whatever it is they happen to have on special. You can't go wrong. You'll become a regular if you visit Florence often enough. (I am.) Impressive wine

selection. My Favorites: Truffle Raviolis and Stuffed Meatballs (these are exceptional, by the way). Seating around a central sushi-bar like counter. Reservations recommended.

MARKETS

CENTRAL MARKET
MERCADO CENTRALE
Piazza del Mercato Centrale 4, + 055 2399798
https://www.mercatocentrale.it/firenze/
This 19th Century iron-and-glass market hall is THE place to go for fresh produce of any kind. The structure itself reminds me slightly of the old iron-and-glass masterpiece that was Penn Station before the idiots in New York blinked and let the powers-that-be pull it down. Restaurant owners in the eateries surrounding the market arrive before anybody else gets out of bed to snag the best of the best. Smart

locals are quick to follow them. Up on the second floor is a Foot Court where you can sample the foods, cheeses, wines from the area surrounding Florence. It's bustling, crowded, hectic and not for the claustrophobic, but it's still a great experience.

FLOWER MARKET
MERCADO DELLE PIANTE
Loggiati de Via Pellicceria
It's only open September through June (and only on Thursdays), and even though you might not be in the market for bunches of flowers or potted plants, this is a wonderful way to spend a few hours strolling among the offerings and reminding yourself how beautiful plants can be. You'll be mixing with thousands of locals out buying items for their homes.

MARKET OF SANT'AMBROSIO
MERCATO SANT'AMBROSIO
Piazza Lorenzo Ghiberti, +39 055 248 0778
www.mercatosantambrogio.it
WEBSITE DOWN AT PRESSTIME
NEIGBORHOOD: Duomo
A less touristy market, this indoor marketplace offers authentic Florentine dishes and an assortment of local products. Vendor booths sell fruits, vegetables, pastries, meat, fish and cheese.
Open Mon-Sat 7am - 2 pm

SAN LORENZO MARKET
MARCHÉ DE SAN LORENZO
Piazza del Mercato Centrale, Firenze FI, +39 055 239 9798
www.mercatocentrale.it/
NEIGBORHOOD: San Lorenzo
This market is actually two separate markets - an indoor market and an outdoor market lining the surrounding streets of the history Mercato Centrale building. The indoor two-level food hall is packed with stalls of fresh produce, local art, leather goods. And a variety of cooking school and artisan stalls.

COOKING SCHOOLS

COOK EAT ITALIAN
Viale Donato Giannotti 49, 055 9064092
http://cookeatitalian.com/
Here the cooking is taught by Manuela, and the experience with her (and we can't forget Simon) couldn't be more different from the super-organized schools like "Cucina" listed just below. You'll go to a small house where you'll learn how to cook a

splendid meal, and then you'll eat it. Wines are pared to the course. Very personal, very lovely time.

THE CUCINA LORENZO DE' MEDICI
Piazza del Mercato Centrale, 334 304 0551
https://cucinaldm.com/en
NEIGHBORHOOD: Santa Maria Novella
Located in the Central Market in Florence, this cooking school offers cooking courses and tastings of the food prepared. Great way to learn food preparation, history of certain dishes and taste the delicious food prepared during class. Most classes last 2-3 hours. They have a slew of widely varied courses to choose from. You work at a station with one other person. Check website for scheduling. Price includes

cooking class, ingredients, final tasting with a glass of wine, water, and an apron with the school logo.

MAMA FLORENCE
Viale Francesco Petrarca 12, + 055 220101
https://www.mamaflorence.com/en
When you come to this wonderful cooking school, they'll serve you coffee and biscotti before teaching you how to make it! (Well, not every class shows you how to make biscotti, just kidding.) The groups here

are small, so there's lots of personal attention from the chefs, who know their stuff, let me tell you. You'll be taught how to make pasta, how to cook it, and when the class is over, the chefs whip up a lovely meal for you to enjoy. If you have even a tiny amount of interest in cooking, this could easily be the highlight of your trip.

INDEX

'

'INO, 18

5

5 E CINQUE, 19

A

Accademia, 6
ALL' ANTICO RISTORI DI CAMBI, 20
ANTICA PASTICCERIA SIENI, 20

ARÀ, 21
ATTRACTIONS & LANDMARKS, 11

B

Bakery, 26, 34
Baptistery, 6
Baptistery of John the Baptist, 12
Bar, 28, 57
Bargello, 6
Bartolucci, 14
Basilica di San Lorenzo, 12
Boboli Gardens, 12
BORGO ANTICO, 22
BRAC, 23

C

Cafe, 24, 61
Café, 23, 58
CAFFE AMERINI, 24
CAFFE CIBREO, 24
CAFFE DELL'ORO, 25
CAFFE RICCHI, 26
Campanile, 12
CANTINETTA DEL VERRAZZANO, 26
CARABÈ, 27
CASA DEL VINO, 28
Cathedral, 6
CENTRAL MARKET, 69
Chocolates, 57
Chocolatier, 20, 31
CIBREO TEATRO DEL SALE, 29
COOK EAT ITALIAN, 73
COOKING SCHOOLS, 3
COQUINARIUS, 29
CUCINA LORENZO DE' MEDICI, 74

CUISINE, 6
CULTURE & ART, 9

D

DA NERBONE, 30
Desserts, 57
DOLCI & DOLCEZZE, 31
Duomo, 10
Duomo of Florence, 10

E

ENOTECA PINCHIORRI, 32

F

FLORENCE'S CENTRAL MARKET, 8
FLOWER MARKET, 70
FOUR SEASONS HOTEL, 42
Frozen Yogurt, 27, 34, 46, 48, 55, 58

G

Galleria dell'Accademia, 10
Galleria dell'Accademia, 10
GELATERIA DEI NERI, 33
GELATERIA GARABE, 9
Gelato, 34, 66
GETTING AROUND, 15
GHIBELLINA FORNO, 34
GILDA, 34
GOLDEN VIEW OPEN BAR, 35
Gucci, 14
GUCCI OSTERIA, 36
GUCCI OSTERIA DA MASSIMO BOTTURA, 36

GURDULU, 37

H

HOSTARIA IL DESCO, 38

I

I DUE FRATELLINI, 39
Ice cream, 46, 55
Ice Cream, 27, 34, 48, 58
IL BORRO, 39
IL CERNACCHINO, 40
IL MERCATO CENTRALE, 41
IL PILAGIO, 42
IL SANTO BEVITORE, 43
Italian, 22, 24, 26, 29, 34, 35, 41, 43, 44, 49, 50, 51, 52, 55, 58, 64

K

KONNUBIO, 44

L

L'OSTERIA DI GIOVANNI, 45
LA BOTTEGA DEL BUON CAFÉ, 9
LA CARRAIA, 46
LA MENAGERE, 47
LA PICCOLA CORTE, 46
LE BOTTEGHE DI LEONARDO, 48
LOBS FISH RESTAURANT, 49

M

MAMA FLORENCE, 75

MANGIAFOCO, 49
MARCHÉ DE SAN LORENZO, 72
MARKET OF SANT'AMBROGIO, 71
MARKETS, 3
Medici Chapel, 12
Mediterranean, 56
MERCADO CENTRALE, 69
MERCADO DELLE PIANTE, 70
MERCATO CENTRALE, 30
Mercato Nuovo on Via Porta Rossa,, 14
MERCATO SANT'AMBROGIO, 71

N

NERBONE, 8

O

OLIO & CONVIVIUM, 50
OSTARIA DEI CENTOPOVERI, 52
OSTERIA CAFFÈ ITALIANO, 51
OSTERIA CINGHIALE BIANCO, 51
OSTERIA DI PASSIGNANO, 53
OSTERIA FRANCESCANA, 53
OSTERIA PEPO, 54

P

Palazzo Pitti, 12
Palazzo Vecchio, 10
Pastries, 31
Pastry, 66
PERCHE NO!, 55
Piazza del Duomo, 12

Piazza della Signoria, 10
Piazza San Lorenzo, 14
Piazzale Michelangelo, 12
Pitti Palace, 10
Pizza, 22, 52, 56
POLPA BURGER TRATTORI, 9
Ponte Vecchio, 13
Prada, 14

R

RINUCCIO 1180, 55
RISTORANTE DA MIMMO, 56
RIVOIRE, 57
ROBIGLIO, 58

S

San Lorenzo Market, 20
SAN LORENZO MARKET, 72
Sandwiches, 18, 39, 40, 59
Santa Croce, 6, 13
Santa Maria Novella, 6
SE STO ON ARNO ROOFTOP, 58
SEI DIVINO, 59
SEMEL, 59
SERGIO GOZZI, 60
SHAKE CAFÈ, 61
SHOPPING, 13
Sicilian, 21, 36, 54
Steakhouse, 41

T

TASTE FLORENCE, 17
TRATTORIA 4 LEONI, 62
TRATTORIA DA ROCCO, 62
TRATTORIA DEL CARMINE, 63
TRATTORIA L'PARIONE, 64
TRATTORIA LA CASALINGA, 64
TRATTORIA MARIO, 8
TRATTORIA MARIONE, 65
TRATTORIA SOSTANZA, 8, 65
Tuscan, 20, 39, 46, 49, 54, 59, 60, 62, 63, 64, 65, 67

U

Uffizi, 6, 10

V

Vegetarian, 19, 23
VIVOLI, 66

W

WESTIN EXCELSIOR, 58
Wine Bar, 51, 67

Z

ZEB, 67

Lightning Source UK Ltd.
Milton Keynes UK
UKHW022231130522
402976UK00012B/1818

9 798201 193751